Power Walking

A Journey to Wholeness

Maxine Bigby Cunningham

POWER WALKING, A Journey to Wholeness
Copyright©2008 by Maxine Bigby Cunningham
All Rights Reserved.

Biblical quotations are from the Holy Bible, New International Version®, Zondervan NIV Study Bible (Fully Revised), © 1985, 1995, 2002 by the Zondervan Corporation, published by Zondervan, Grand Rapids, Michigan 49530, U.S.A.

Formatting by
Rend Graphics, Summerville, South Carolina

Art Designs:
Ruby, The Three of Us, Nappy Headed Self, Where Three are Gathered, Zoe
Used with permission of Artist:
Sharon D. Cope of Sharon D. Cope, Inc.,
Pensacola, Florida

Publisher:
BookSurge Publishing, North Charleston, South Carolina

Cunningham, Maxine Bigby, 1948 –
   Power Walking: A Journey to Wholeness
   p. cm.

Library of Congress Control Number 2007907799

ISBN Number 9781419643910

Dedication

This book is dedicated to my parents,
Maxwell Miles and Pauline Smith Bigby

And to my children,
Wesley Ernest and Theresa Annette Cunningham

Contents

Acknowledgements

I am grateful to many. I acknowledge:

My ancestors – they passed on a love of storytelling. They say that folks, both Black and White, came from miles around, to hear tales by my great, great uncle, Uncle Sam. Uncle Sam was an ex-slave, my mother's kinship care giver, a minister, and a storyteller in the African Griot tradition. My mother did not simply read books to her children, her grandchildren, and everybody else's children; she performed the stories with fervor and animation. And Lord knows that my Aunt Pearl's storytelling was a much cherished time at Christmas family gatherings.

My twin, Pauline – she prayed constantly for me, willing me to "Be Alive" and in some sense, she shared each step on this journey.

My children, Wes and Miss T – they gave me reasons for getting back on my feet whenever I fell and they supported me in taking steps, unsteady though they were, while I learned to walk differently.

My niece and god daughter, Monica – she encouraged and uplifted me as I persevered in completing each task in the writing and publishing processes.

My husband, Ernest – he allowed me the time and the space to write. While it is different from the way it used to be, love remains still.

My cousin, Ella Grace – she gave me a resting place when I was homeless and she reviewed my early draft.

My Sister Friends, Candace, Jackie, Carolyn, Jai, Diana, Miriam, Virginia, Madelyn R., Madelyn B., Francine, Evelyn, and Shelley– they walked along side me on the journey.

My Women's Ministry at Pleasant Hope Baptist Church – these Sisters in Christ surrounded me with love and inspired the first poem that I shared publicly, "Transformation".

My editor, Clara Anthony - she untiringly guided and assisted this new author.

My acupuncturist, Rabab Al-Amin – she energized my body and my spirit.

My therapist, Janice E. Stevenson – she coached me in discovering the power of choice.

To God I give all the praise.

Preface

I was among the "walking wounded". I did not know who I was. A walking zombie is an apt description - limping through a fog, clueless, proceeding on cruise control, moving robotically, numb...

No wonder I kept walking into things.
No wonder I kept falling down.
No wonder I kept losing consciousness.

I had gone to the mall to have my prescription filled for new eyeglasses. I had an hour's wait. It had been a long day; I felt tired and drained. If I sat on a bench, I might drift to sleep. So I decided to just walk … to stroll around the mall

As I passed by a women's apparel shop, I saw a reflection in the display window, amidst the beautiful clothes adorning the manikins. It was an image of a middle aged woman. Her coat was oversized, hanging down to her ankles, past her wrists, over her shoulders. Her shoes were not at all fashionable.

With a jolt, I realized that this apparition was a reflection of me. "That image doesn't look the way I feel," thought I; "at least not the way I want to be seen. There is no pep in her step; no sparkle in her eyes; no glow on her face. She looks sooo sad. No Joy."

I was passing among people – strangers - whom I did not know. I was moving among colleagues and associates – friends - who did not know me. I was sauntering among cousins and children – family – who knew the things that I did but did not know who I am. I was meandering, rambling, wandering among all kinds of folks

It hurt me to see the hurt in me. Did anyone hear the shallowness in my laughter, see the emptiness of my gaze, or perceive the hollowness of my spirit? I saw a sick woman. In that reflecting glass, I saw brokenness. While strolling, I decided that it was time…past time to change this picture.

This collection of writings documents a journey to wholeness.
The writing was therapeutic.
The sharing is celebratory

Prologue

I have a history of fainting.

Do you not know? Have you not heard? The LORD is the everlasting God, the Creator of the ends of the earth. He will not grow tired or weary, and his understanding no one can fathom.

He gives strength to the weary and increases the power of the weak.

Even youths grow tired and weary, and young men stumble and fall;

But those who hope in the LORD will renew their strength. They will soar on wings like eagles; they will run and not grow weary, they will walk and not be faint.

Isaiah 40:28-33 (NIV)

WALK

> Saunter, tread, amble, meander,
> Step, move, go
> Stride, pace, march, hike,
> Stroll, travel, progress

FAINT

> Fade, wane, abate, recede
> Fail, sleep, pass out
> Falter, stumble, wobble, hesitate,
> Fall, collapse, black-out
>
> Give way, give up, give in, give out

My fainting is history.

Introduction

Sunday, January 7, 1997, was a crisp but sunny wintry day. That was outside. Inside, my house was dark. My spouse and I engaged in an intense conversation about relationships, not ours but with someone else who was dear to us both. Continuing an ongoing, seemingly endless debate, we each held firm to our disparate positions. I knew there was more to be said, but I was running late for church service. As I walked out the door, I retorted angrily, pleased that I had gotten in the last word. I had worked myself into such frenzy that, as I turned the ignition in the car, I felt a headache coming on. It would get better, I thought; I just needed to take a few deep breaths. I was mistaken.

The headache got worse. My spouse had joined me at church, seated a few pews behind where I sat. After the altar call, I whispered to him that I felt ill, but I believed that I could make it through the worship service. What I was feeling in my head grew to more than an ache – it had become a burning, tortuous, excruciating pain. I felt dizzy, nauseous and light-headed. I had to leave right then. Just moments before the benediction was pronounced, I stepped over several people and moved towards the back of the sanctuary. Before I reached the doors, my vision dimmed, my feet faltered and I felt my knees buckle. Everything went dark.

I felt a cool breeze. Someone was fanning. On my back, I gazed up at my husband standing at my feet. I saw the church nurses on each side; I heard the Pastor leading the congregation in prayer; he then proceeded to the rear of the sanctuary, knelt beside me, held my hand and prayed in a soft, fervent tone. Months later I would learn that a congregant had caught me before I hit the floor, softening my fall.

By the time the ambulance transported me to the hospital emergency room, my speech was garbled. I am told that the right side of my face was distorted - drooping eye, twisted mouth, and

sagging cheek. In the hospital emergency room, there were many...
many anxious moments, many diagnostic tests, and many visits
from family and church friends. Several hours after my arrival, the
doctor returned with the results from the tests: "You have had a
transient ischemic attack", he said, "a mild, temporary stroke". It
was not critical, but very serious. That night, with measured steps,
I exited the hospital on my feet. Over the next two years, I would
experience other fainting incidents.

Friday, March 23, 1997, was a warm spring-like day, sunny and bright.
I embraced the peacefulness of this day which I was spending at
home. I sat at the kitchen table gazing out the window. The radio
played in the background. The host announced that he would
be interviewing the author of a new book, Risk and Other Four
Letter Words. My interest peaked by the title, the idea occurred
to me that I could write my own book, a book just for me. Cutting
off the radio, I picked up a bound composition book, walked into
my back yard, sat on the concrete bench under a large apple tree,
and I began to write. Despite my taking this and other occasional
"mental health days", the fainting incidents continued.

The next time that I fainted was in a Philadelphia hotel. I was
to attend a work-related meeting with federal fair housing
investigators from across the country. The Office which I managed
was responsible for technical oversight of the investigators'
performance. The preceding evening, one of my favorite colleagues
and I chatted as we exercised, walking side by side on treadmills. It
had been a long day, so I supposed that the sudden light headiness I
felt was due to fatigue. I pressed the "Cool Down" button, came to
a stop and stepped off the equipment. For a few minutes, I sat in a
nearby chair before proceeding to my guest room. Feeling better,
I got up, took a few steps and then fainted. There was another trip
by ambulance to a hospital emergency room. I later returned to
the hotel with instructions not to be alone for the remainder of
the night and to rest in bed all of the following day. This time the
diagnosis was an anxiety attack.

Yet another incident occurred in Williamsburg where my husband and I were on vacation. Always visiting historical sites on our travels, the two of us stood in the rear of a landmark Court House, witnessing a dramatic rendition of a historic trial. It was crowded and it was sweltering hot. I remember wiping my sweaty brow and leaning against the wall. When the presentation concluded, tour guides ushered us spectators out the door so that the next group could enter. However, I was afraid to move. My legs felt like jelly, my eyes rolled to the back of my head, and I started to slide down the wall. Someone noticed and pulled me up before I hit the floor. Quickly escorted to an adjacent, cooler room, I felt like I was about to pass out. This marked the third trip by ambulance to an emergency room due to a "fainting spell". The diagnosis this time was heat exhaustion.

The next two incidents did not require trips to the hospital. Nonetheless they were pieces of a disquieting and disconcerting pattern. It was another year and another vacation. We were attending my husband's family reunion in North Carolina. We stood chatting with cousins in the backyard garden where family and friends had gathered. I began to feel ill, so I retreated inside to the cool of the family room. I stretched out on a recliner. Beginning to swoon, I closed my eyes and took deep breaths. Noticing that I was perspiring profusely, someone called my husband in from the garden; he wiped my brow, handed me a glass of ice water, and placed a cold towel on my forehead. I rested and an hour later, I was able to re-engage with the family. I was grateful that I had clung to consciousness.

The last fainting episode occurred in the Fitness Center at the Office. Exercising early in the morning, I was looking forward to the Performance Awards Ceremony scheduled later that day. The top Administrator would present awards to staff for outstanding performance and jobs well done. Having completed my workout, I headed for the shower, but while crossing the room, I felt weak. Pausing on my way out, I asked that the Center Director take my blood pressure. It was high; so she told me to lie on a floor mat, and she elevated my head. Fifteen minutes later I felt better; I stood up. As I got on my feet, my head started to swim, my knees buckled, and I crumpled to the floor. Responding to an emergency call, nurses helped me into a wheel chair and whisked me to a bed in the Health Unit. A close colleague visited me, admonishing me for not taking proper care of myself. Eventually, I was able to get up, shower and dress in time for the Ceremony.

Every member of my staff received recognition. I was so proud of them. As the Ceremony neared a close, I waited with anticipation. The program ended. No one had called my name, beckoning me to come forward for recognition and applause. Folks began to whisper, averting their eyes from mine as they departed from the Auditorium. I arduously pasted a smile on my face, graciously extended my hand, and enthusiastically congratulated the award recipients. Some persons told me that it was not fair that I received no award; most said nothing.

I did not want to believe it. Thus, I denied the clear message sent by my supervisors that they believed the outstanding accomplishments of my Office were despite my personal contributions and leadership in exceeding all program goals. More than a slight, the lack of recognition was a slap that made my head spin and left me with a clear, if invisible, scar. For a few weeks I managed to stay on my feet. My work days were endless; my nights were sleepless. Not surprisingly, I exhibited symptoms of sleep deprivation. Based on my doctor's recommendation, I reduced my work week from five to four days. That was not enough.

I fell into a deeper state of dis-ease. I had issues – mental, emotional, physical and spiritual. Still, I did not want to leave my job and bring my career to a close. My doctors and I compromised. I took three months of sick leave; it was a period for rest and restoration from a high level, high stressed job. While I was away, my colleague and friend, despite warning me about the risk of working too hard, died in her bed from a massive heart attack. My heart ached. Her death was my wake-up call.

About two weeks before the scheduled return to my job, my daughter called to say that she had found a lump in her breast. She asked that I come be with her when she underwent a surgical procedure for a biopsy. Her maternal grandmother, had a double mastectomy, and she died when the cancer spread uncontrollably throughout her bones and organs. My daughter was scared and so was I. On top of everything else, my marriage was falling apart. The morning that I was to depart, I had a panic attack. Walking hastily, I fell as I turned the corner around the island in the kitchen. I just lay on the floor for minutes, catching my breath. My ankle hurt so badly that I could not rise on my own.

Nonetheless, I did not even consider changing my travel plans, and I had too much to get done to pause for a trip to the hospital emergency room. That evening, I hobbled onto a train for a 12-hour ride to Atlanta.

Arriving in Atlanta, I rented a car and readied myself to assume the role of care-giver for my daughter. However, two days later, the throbbing pain from that "sprained" ankle was so severe that I reverted to a child's method of getting around; I crawled. Despite protests, my daughter insisted on taking me to the neighborhood medical facility. I was seen by a Black woman physician. Looking at the x-rays, she said to me, "Sister, you done broke every bone that attaches the left femur to your ankle." I hobbled out on crutches with an appointment to see an orthopedic surgeon the next morning. My daughter's biopsy was scheduled for that afternoon.

In the morning the orthopedic surgeon scheduled my surgery for the following day and ordered a series of immediate "pre-operative procedures". Now how was I going to take care of my daughter? I mean, that was why I was in Atlanta, right? Fortunately my daughter's surgery was within the same medical complex. The pre-operative tests took longer than expected, my ambulatory speed was slow; and the distance was great between the orthopedic and the general surgery wings of the medical center.

Some merciful soul saw me teetering; he found a wheel chair and pushed me to the doctor's office where I was joining my daughter. By the time I arrived, my daughter had been called to the surgical room and she already was on the operating table. In response to my frantic plea, the doctor allowed me a moment just outside of the operating room so that I could see my daughter and speak with him. I was not able to kiss her, but she saw me and knew that I had arrived. The tumor was benign. That fall three days earlier almost caused me to miss my purpose.

I remained in Atlanta, alone, in a motel for three weeks, recuperating from the leg surgery, and deciding whether I wanted to go back home. I returned to my residence, I returned to my husband, and I returned to my job. A few months later, after a fairly illustrious career in federal service, I retired. The year was 1999.

I enjoyed the leisurely, yet full days of my early retirement. Among other things, I enjoyed writing in my bound composition book, writings that were just for me. I believe that every creative writer is a dreamer. As a college freshman, I envisioned a career as a manager in a community economic development organization located in an African American, low incomes community similar to the one in which I grew up. To my surprise, I received an unsolicited offer for such a position. With fervor I launched into this new career. Again, I lost my balance. This time, curled up in a ball, writhing with pain. Another trip I made to the emergency room of a hospital, this time in the wee hours of the morning. Diagnosed with an intestinal blockage, I went from the emergency room to the operating room. After nearly three years, I left another job that I loved that did not love me back. Time had passed and it was now 2002.

It was not my original intent to share this collection of writings. I have presented selections of poetry and prose to individuals who touched my life and to persons whose paths crossed with mine. I hoped the writings would be messages of encouragement and expressions of caring. I was astonished when I received requests to compose poems for special occasions and for specific individuals. Then, someone suggested that I publish a book. The year was 2004.

In this collection of writings, I use as a major metaphor the process of learning how to walk. You will see frequent references to fainting/falling and to walking. These words are illustrative of the" downs" and the "ups" along my life's journey. I believe that the stages of learning how to walk metaphorically describe how each of us lives - physically, emotionally, mentally, and spiritually. Fainting connotes weakness, unsteadiness, and unconsciousness. On the other hand, walking connotes movement, energy, and purpose. No one learns to walk without falling, without getting back up after falling, without taking small steps before hitting a stride. Walking requires practice, and that means discipline. Physically, learning to walk is a developmental process. The same is true for the processes which activate the heart, mind and the spirit.

The walking process is depicted as having four stages: getting on your feet, taking baby steps; staying on your feet, and in due course, acquiring a different, assured kind of walk. Depending on its use and context, grammatically the word "walk" is a noun or a verb: a walk is thing, a state of being; "to walk" is to act, to reach, and to perform. The word has seeming contradictions: walk may mean to come or to go; to enter or to depart. This word conveys diverse levels of consciousness: to wander, to stroll, and to march. This word suggests various degrees of strength: to amble, to trudge, and to hike. This word communicates different levels of competencies: to plod, to trek, and to live. The kind of walk that I seek is movement which is mindful, deliberate, and focused.

When learning to walk, falling is part of the process. Falling may leave "telltale" signs, like bumps, bruises, and scars. Falling may keep us in a familiar yet unwholesome place – where we resided before we got to our feet and took those baby steps forward. Falling may land us in an unfamiliar although healthy space – where we've never dwelt. We can take heart that falling is only part of the process and not the culmination of our efforts. I began a re-directed journey when I fainted as a result of the mild stroke. I intuitively knew that there was something wrong with how I was walking. I had to learn a different kind of walk. I prayed that in the process, I would not lose consciousness... again.

I believe that my frequent fainting/falling incidents were signs of a life which lacked authenticity, balance and meaning. My living was tied up by fear. Physically, emotionally, and spiritually I had been running and I was flatly exhausted. After a long while, I accepted the reality that I was broken in many places and in many spaces. Restoration would require relaxation, meditation, physical exercise, spiritual sit-ups (trusting what I could not see) and sleep, lots of rest. Steeped in denial, I had failed to heed warning signs because I viewed yielding as a sign of weakness. I had yet to learn that persistence is not the same as perseverance under God's grace. I had been stubborn. I had been obstinate. I had been dwelling in a state of mindlessness. I lacked the focus which emanates from centering on those things which integrate the brain, heart and soul. I wanted to be whole.

Walking is both a daily experience and a life-time journey. When I get on my feet, I experience pulling up as a strength-building exercise. When I take a step, I experience movement as aerobic training. When I stay on my feet, I experience balance as the result of proper breathing, posture, and focus. I learned that I can walk and not be faint. Now, I walk differently. I am more prayerful, mindful, thankful, and joyful. Understanding that my God did not give me the spirit of fear, now I am power walking!

Getting on my Feet

He lifted me out of the slimy pit, out of the mud and mire; he set my feet on a rock and gave me a firm place to stand.

Psalm 40:2 (NIV)

Do not be anxious about anything, but in everything, by prayer and petition, with thanksgiving, present your requests to God.

Philippians 4:6 (NIV)

Once a child begins to roll over, we eagerly anticipate the day that the child will, on her own strength, get up on her feet. We prepare her: holding her up securely as she jumps, feet never leaving our laps; holding her tightly as her feet lift slightly, prancing from one foot to the other; we laugh, she laughs.

Once a child learns to stand and then to walk, falls are expected. These "short people" do not have far to fall and quickly "re-group" and get up once more. The child receives encouragement and cheers. Later in life, falling can be infinitely more challenging than during the childhood rehearsal.

As an adult, I have lain sprawled on the ground, crouched in a corner, curled upon a bed. I was not in an upright position. I had walked before and hoped that with practice, I would walk once more. I began by getting on my feet – again.

unbelief

The most difficult part

about getting on my feet

is believing that I can.

Lord, help me overcome my unbelief.

days

I have a mental illness

which can be very debilitating.

I have some days that are very good and

I have some days that are not so good.

BUT

I thank GOD that I have days

...and they are all

G O O D!

I Cry

It is not that I am not heard,
But that I am not understood.

It is not that I am not noticed,
But that I am not acknowledged.

It is not that I am alone,
But that I am lonely.

It is not that no one cares,
But that no one trusts.

It is not that I feel hurt,
But that I know pain.

It is not that I have no hope,
But that still, I must hope.

It is not that others expect nothing,
But that others praise not.

It is not the message that frightens me,
But the voice is so angry and yet so anxious.

Sometimes with deep groans,
Sometimes with silent tears,
I Cry.

For those who are harmed and hurt;
For those who afflict harm and hurt,
I Cry.

Tears can be cleansing.
Tears can be healing.
So, I Cry.

SCARS

Scars are marks left by the healing of injured tissue. Injuries have seen and unseen causes.

Some scars are caused by searing heat and others by freezing cold. Some scars are very large, and others are barely perceptible. Some scars mask self-inflicted cuts and others cover gashes inflicted by others. Some scars are due to incisions which provided access for removal of diseased, infected or harmful tissues. All scars result from contact with something sharp.

Scars are marks of pain; scars are signs of healing. It depends on how you look at it.

What do you see?

Physical Pain or Emotional Tear?

An Opening or a Closure?

Visible Blemish or Invisible Wound?

Covered Defect or Exposed Deformity?

Superficial Scratch or Deep Indentation?

Death Escaped or Existence Spared?

Life Threatened or Life Saved?

Hurt Inestimable or Healing Immeasurable?

Secret Unveiled or Testimony Untold?

Struggle Fought or Victory Won?

T. L. C.

Ever been so tired that you just could not get out of bed?
Ever been so sick that you would not get out of bed?
Ever feel so incapacitated that you were clearly bed-ridden?
Ahhh...these are the days when all you want is someone to tenderly
nurse you to good health with some TLC,

Tender

Loving

Care

Ever been so dismayed that you just decided to stay in bed?
Ever been so disheartened that you did not care if you ever got out of
bed?
Ever been so distraught that you jut did not feel it was worth getting out
of bed?
Ohhh...these are the days when all you need is someone to compassionately
speak to your inner strength with some TLC,

Tough

Love

Communication

"Grace" and other Five Letter Words

Growing up in a Southern Baptist church and in a devout Christian family, references to God's "grace" and "mercy" were common. Although I could not offer precise definitions, I understood that these two five - letter words applied to the ways that God shields us from hurt, harm and danger. The spiritual meaning of the number "5" is "Grace". Other five-letter words remind us of God's unmerited favor.

Some words communicate existence:
Alive
Aware
Being
Birth
Renew

Some words contain memories:
Child
Music
Scent
Smile
Voice

Some words convey feelings:
Bliss
Happy
Honor
Peace
Quiet

Some words conjure up visions:
Color
Dream
Image
Stars
Water

Some words call to action:
Dance
Plant
Reach
Teach
Write

Some words define our relationship with God:
Bless
Blood
Loved
Mercy
Whole

REACH

REACH
> out for the help of others.

REACH
> back to those proven practices for serenity and courage.

REACH
> forward with hope and faith.

REACH
> up knowing that I AM here Always.

UP

FOCUS
Converge Up
Close Up
Clean Up
Clear Up

SURRENDER
Listen Up
Let Up
Look Up
Lift Up

MOVE
Get Up
Grab Up
Grow Up
Go Up

HOLY-DAYS

Let's embrace the Blessings of this Season of Holy-Days
Peace, Joy and Love

Peace upon Birth: the New Born,
the Now Reborn; the Not yet Born.

Joy of Connection: Creator, Community, Cousins.

Love in the Lord, Light, Life.

Hmmm

I think that I will live as if each day is HOLY.

WALKING PARTNER

It is February 2002. I occupy a room on the fourth floor of Sinai Hospital. The time is between midnight and dawn. The only light peeps under the door from the corridor. While my roommate slumbers, sleep escapes me. Rest has taken flight. Nothing moves; even time stands still. People seem so far away. During my hospitalization, family, friends, doctors, nurses and staff have entered and exited my physical space in this room. I have tried to cooperate, to be a "good" patient.

I think back over the past several days. It has been more than a week now. I have been lying in the bed, sitting by the window looking out at nothing in particular, and, occasionally, to pacify the pushy nurses, I have shuffled down the corridors. I endured stares from those who counted the six bags hanging from the pole I pushed in front of me. The pole and I have become inseparable, connected by intravenous tubes of liquids sustaining my life. I am not critically ill, but I am not well. Healing is slow, so I wait. I wait for restoration of my body, responsiveness of my mind, revival of my spirit.

So, I try talking to myself. I find no words that soothe my spirit. I do not want to spend the night in sedentary lifelessness. What was I to do? If I turned on the lights or TV, I might startle my roommate into wakefulness. On the other hand, if I walk the corridor at this ungodly hour, the nurses would "write me up" and the doctors would wonder about that notation in my chart.

Walking is the prescription I had received days before. The exercise, they said, would help me heal – my internal organs recover their effectiveness, my muscles regain their strength; my eyes recapture their light. Because I had not wanted to walk alone, I limited my activity. For me, exercise is a social activity. If only I had a walking partner.

At this moment, as I lie awake between the night and the morning, the days seem endless, hours countless and minutes incalculable. I feel as if I dwell in open isolation. I feel as if there is no one to listen and no one with whom I can talk. Just as well. Words catch in my throat.

Near dawn I feel another's presence with me. As if coming from far off, I hear "God Is".
I petition: Lord, Mercy, Sorry, Please, Jesus
I plea: My Lord. Have mercy. Forgive me. Guide me. Jesus Christ.
I pray: Oh Merciful God. Heal Me Now. Help me Rise. Order My Steps. Walk with me.

Close to daybreak, I feel comforted. I find sleep. In the morning, the sun shines, inner voices sing. I rise from the bed without coaxing. On this day, I spend only a few moments in the chair by the window. Time seems to fly. All day long, I walk the corridors, my Walking Partner and me.

A few days later, I returned home. Now, as I start each day, I greet my Walking Partner. Once I am on my feet, I am assured that I will not walk alone.

Taking Baby Steps

If the Lord delights in a man's way, he makes his steps firm.
Psalm 37:23 (NIV)

Finally brothers, whatever is true, whatever is pure, whatever is lovely, whatever is admirable -if anything is excellent or praiseworthy – think about such things.
Philippians 4:8 (NIV)

She had visited the Office before. In the midst of a crisis, she had come seeking help in getting help for a relative. This time, she had come for herself. She decided to "put herself in therapy". A welcoming voice said, "Good Evening". She rose from the chair in the reception area, and with tentative, tottering steps, she entered the therapist's inner office.

The new client, although she always prepared detailed agendas prior to any planned meeting, had brought no list, no pen and no paper to this meeting. Although she never wore much make-up, she had taken care to freshen up her lipstick and blush. Although she spoke before people daily, she now found it difficult to articulate fluently or eloquently to the one woman who sat across from her.

The therapist asked about the relative about whom the client had first sought help. Then looking into the eyes of the one who sat before her, the therapist said, "I knew that you would be back." Although silent, the new client must have looked pained because her eyes filled with tears. She heard the question, "Where does it hurt?" She pointed to her stomach, next to her chest, and lastly to her throat. What does it feel like? The reply was an utterance of few words, "tight, heavy, and closed".

The therapist placed a box of crayons and a sheet of white paper in front of the client and instructed the client, who was right-handed, to choose a color and then draw with her left hand. After 15 minutes or so, the client timidly extended her arm, returning the paper with what looked to her like scribble-scrabble. The therapist reached out for the paper; studied the picture, then smiled. The appraisal was a single word, "Good".

The therapist stood. The new client guest slowly rose from her seat. Their time together was momentarily at an end. Notwithstanding outward appearance, the client had entered like a toddler, not crawling yet clinging, not trusting her ability to walk hands free. Feeling validated by the assessment of her drawing, she willed her feet to move towards the door. She felt like a baby who, without holding on, had taken her first steps.

A Child's Prayer

O God who is in Heaven, You are Holy.

Protect me, my family, my friends, and everyone.

Please forgive me when I do not obey my parents or You, God.

I thank you for my food, my clothes, and my home.

I thank you for Jesus Christ who died on the cross for my sins.

I thank you for the promise that I will see Grandma again in heaven.

Lord, I am so glad that you love me; I love you too.

I pray in Jesus' name.

AMEN.

ANTICIPATING

HOPING

PRAYING

PLANTING

PLANNING

TRUSTING

WAITING

EXPECTING

21

WHEREVER

No matter how far or close
No matter how crowded or sparse
No matter how big or small
No matter how luxurious or scarce
No matter how loud or quiet

I can't seem to
Leave, hide, vanish, or escape
Me.

Regardless
Despite
Nonetheless

Me just keeps
Showing up,

Everywhere...wherever "I be".

WHAT I LEARNED TODAY
Thursday, September 1, 2005

If I look for the lesson in my experiences, however painful or joyful they may be, I will stay connected to God; I will maintain balance – physically, mentally, emotionally and spiritually; I will remain whole.

I can change my mind. God allows U-turns. My responsibility is to keep the opening and not close the circle, or I will wind up in the same place that I left – the place that I walked away from.

When my therapist says that she will see me next Thursday at 10:00 a.m. what she really means is that God willing, she promises to do her best to see me next Thursday at 10:00 in the morning. The promise is in the intent, not the accomplished deed. Only God can always keep promises, and even then the promise is kept on God's time schedule and in a manner that is according to God's will. I wait, knowing that the promise will be fulfilled, praying that I will recognize its fulfillment, and being grateful for the knowing.

Because I know better, I can do better by my children. By letting them make their own decisions, plans, mistakes, successes, and by not rescuing them from themselves, I nurture, support and love them...I allow them to explore, learn and be who they are.

Pain and disappointment do not have to define my day.

When I return to my house, when I approach the street, when I turn the key in the door, when I walk into the foyer... before taking each step, first, I will pray.

I can tell people what I need; it is empowering, not selfish or inconsiderate.

I am responsible for my own happiness – no one else, just me.

I can experience the power of choice every day.

DAUGHTERS' LOVE

I was a young teenager, perhaps 13 or 14 years old. My mother was standing at the kitchen counter, preparing a meal no doubt. I was mad because she would not give me permission to do something that I wanted to do. I no longer remember what that "something" was. I was furious I raised my voice, stormed out of the kitchen and stomping up the stairs to my room, I looked down at her and shouted, "You don't love me!" I wanted to hurt her. She looked up at me, eyes welled up with tears. I remember the look of pain entwined with an expression of deep love for me. Although I really loved her too, I could not take back my words.

I was a 40-something mother with a teen-age daughter. It seemed that lately we could not have a conversation that was not an argument. After an exchange of words, she went to her room, sulking, I thought. I went to the kitchen to prepare the evening meal. I was standing at the kitchen counter. Silently and suddenly, she entered the kitchen and picked up a long, sharp butcher knife. She yelled at me, right up in my face, punctuating each remark with a jab to the woodblock cutting board, crying despite her obvious rage. I stood motionless, my breath became shallow; I felt and heard her hatred and her grief. I said nothing. As silently and a suddenly as she had entered the kitchen, my daughter returned the knife to the counter and walked back to her room. As I stared at her back, the well of tears overflowed, streaming down my face. I could not vocalize three simple words, "I love you. " My daughter says that she has no memory of this incident.

Is rage connected to feeling unloved?

TALKING TO MYSELF

I talk to myself …
As I stand by myself
In the midst of a crowd
Among strangers
While mingling with friends
Amid family

I talk to myself daily.
It is important that I remember.
It is vital that I recognize.
It is crucial that I recall.
It is essential that I realize.

I talk to myself as a reminder.
I am special.
I am unique.
I am precious.
I am lovable.
I am alive.

LOVE SELF

Love is an action word and it connotes action on the part of the lover. I have found a model by studying how God expresses love for me. This model shows me how to express love to others and to myself.

When I love myself I am

Caring. I give as much consideration to my needs as to the wants of others.

Communicative. I listen to my fears and speak love into my spirit.

Disciplined. I set boundaries for behaviors and energies that I allow into my space and I accept the consequences of failing to say "NO" when I should.

Patient. I suffer through uncomfortable situations and places which are transitions or transitory.

Truthful. I stay out of denial, living life with honesty and authenticity.

Forgiving. I pardon myself, believing that if God can show me mercy, certainly I can leave behind each "should have", "would have", and "could have" in my past.

Compassionate. I comfort myself with a favorite scripture, song, or piece of chocolate candy.

Empowered. I embrace God's will as my safe place and Jesus as my joy's center.

ORDER STEPS IN THE WORD

ORDER:

Obey God's WORD.
Read and study God's WORD.
Do God's Will as inspired by the WORD.
Express God's Love as commanded in the WORD.
Reflect God's Image described in the WORD.

S
P
E
T
S

In the

WORD:

Wisdom
Order
Righteousness
Direction

Staying on my Feet

My steps have held to your paths; my feet have not slipped.
Psalm 17:5 (NIV)

I can do everything through him who gives me strength.
Philippians 4:13 (NIV)

I was about 12 years old. It was a Saturday afternoon in summertime. Mama was in the kitchen, sitting in the chair with the black metal frame and red leathery seat and back covers. Our neighbor was "doing" Mama's hair. I could see steam rise from the straightening comb and hear sizzle as the comb was pulled through my Mama's hair. They engaged in women talk about their children, church happenings and those sorts of thing. It was all part of the Black woman's ritual of maintaining an adorning crown.

I asked Mama for permission to do something – I no longer recall what. Mama said "No." Perhaps it was because I never considered going against her decision, I became "hopping mad". In the words of grown folks, I began to "smell myself". Yelling at Mama, accusing her of, let's just say, being unfair, unreasonable, and just plain wrong. She just sat there as the words tumbled out of my mouth. To make my feelings perfectly clear, I said, "D_ _ n you".

Well, I never saw her eyes flare. I never saw her rise from the chair. I never saw her move towards me. She did not say one word. The next thing I knew, I was holding the side of my face, pained from the slap she had just delivered, like a bolt of lightening, so strong it knocked me off my feet.

Sprawled on the floor, I looked up at Mama, my mouth hung open. I was speechless. She was sitting in the chair, looking at down at me with eyes intolerant of disrespect; and with a facial expression commanding deference. I was stunned. She had my attention. Saying not another word, I got back on my feet and left the kitchen. It was clear that if I were to stay on my feet, something would have to change. That "something" would be me.

In my day, the phrase "four-letter words" was a euphemism for profanity, "cuss" (curse) words we called them: "d_ _n, f_ _k, b_ _l, s_ _t". These words were obscene, evil, and sacrilegious. In those days, on the air waves we heard these words as "beeps"; in cartoons, we read the words as "x#*%"; in the newspapers, these words were omitted but denoted as "expletive deleted". These words were abusive and condemning; these words were sharp and intending to hurt. These words really did not so much imply the unworthiness of their target, as much as they imparted the despair of the human who uttered those words.

Today, God speaks to me in four-letter words. A whisper: "pray"; a command: "obey"; a directive: "move"; a proclamation: "sing". When I stumble, falter or stagger, I listen for God's 4-letter words so that I can stay on my feet.

UNSAID
An Apology

I said that I was sorry for fleeing
  instead of staying with you.
I said that I was sorry for hearing
  instead of listening to you.
I said that I was sorry for taking consolation
  instead of giving comfort.
I said that I was sorry for hiding
  instead of confronting truth.

I am sorry that I did not hug you right and right often.

I said that I was sorry for shields
  that left you without protection.
I said that I was sorry for dysfunctions
  that left you without peacefulness.
I said that I was sorry for defensiveness
  that left you without trust.
I said that I was sorry for fears
  that left you without love.

I am sorry that I did not love you as much as you deserved.

But there was something left unsaid.
Have I ever asked you?
Can I yet ask you?
I ask you now.

I ask for your forgiveness.

DOING TIME

By adolescence, and certainly by adulthood, we have experienced consequences for poor judgment and bad decisions. We have learned at least some of the lessons of life. However, rarely do we learn it all from our initial "mis-steps". We act out, behaving in ways, while outside the legal system, might still be called "criminal".

We sulk:
> Cutting our eyes, putting hands on our hips, turning our head away, extending our arm and pronouncing, "Speak to the Hand"

We rebel:
> Intellectualizing, rationalizing, fantasizing, and dramatizing why our way is better than The Way

We throw temper tantrums:
> Kicking, screaming, swinging and hitting, stretching out on the floor and pounding the floor with our fists

We threaten to leave:
> Thinking the pain will hurt those whom we leave behind more than we are hurting ourselves

Then, someone with greater authority steps in and interrupts our lives as we were living it. Sentenced for transgressions of following Another Way, we must do time.

Time AWAY
> May be a hospital bed or a jail cell

Time OFF
> No deadlines, no distractions

Time FOR
> Rest and stillness

Time TO
> Pray and praise

Time IN
> Meditation and reflection

Time WITH
> Self and truth

WONDER DRUG

This pain is so great. I believe that the only relief is a wonder drug.

What triggers the pain?
Confusion produces a headache. No direction
Commotion causes a lower backache. No peace
Chaos guarantees a stomach ache. No order
Concern begets a sore throat. No voice
Conspiracy ignites blindness. No foresight
Perhaps I can ignore the body signals.

Where is the pain?
My whole body hurts, from head to toe, both inside and out.
My head spins. My eyesight blurs. My neck tightens.
My back aches. My muscles tire. My joints stiffen.
My ears ring. My throat throbs. My stomach churns.
My knees puff up. My ankles puff out. My feet swell up.
Perhaps I can sleep to deaden the distressing sensations.

Who can I call for relief?
My mother would rub my feet if she still lived on earth.
My twin would rub my stomach if she lived in town.
My physician would take my temperature if he were in his Office today.
My acupuncturist would make the energy flow if she were giving treatments this day.
My mental health care providers would engage me in talk therapy.
Perhaps I can call a home delivery pharmacist for an "over the counter" remedy.

Why can't they package a body-soul medication?
There has to be a liquid formula.
There must be an encapsulated powder.
There should be a pill.
There ought to be an herbal mixture.
There is supposed to be an intravenous solution.
Perhaps I can seek health generating alternatives.

How could I concoct my own "drug"?
Memorization - I will recall the words of Holy Scripture hidden in my heart.
Meditation - I will practice daily.
Music - I will enjoy every day.
Movements – I will dance today.
Moments - I will cherish each one.
Perhaps I can.

I Wonder.

PROBLEM SOLVING

Problem Statement: *How do I find balance in my life?*

Background: *Lack of balance has characterized much of my life. The consequences of a lack of balance are clear – stumbling, falling, and fainting, both literally and figuratively.*

Task: *Determine the proper ingredients for balanced living.*

SOLUTION:

Study the Bible, meditate, and pray.

Open space and un-clutter the physical environment.

Lie down, read, write, and sleep.

Understand when and how to say "No".

Take time for exercising and gazing upon nature.

Inquire within self for the "next" steps.

Order my days to develop discipline and focus.

Nurture myself with good food, good friends, and good fun.

CHOICES

<u>Key</u>

Thundering in my head: The expectation outside of myself
Whispering in my heart: The option available but not always discerned
CHOOSING: The action sometimes uncomfortable but always empowering

Work until it is perfect. There is blame and shame in imperfection.
I don't have to work until breathless, no matter how urgent it seems.
BREATHE: Exhale the panic; inhale God's power; get help.

You should be able to do "it".
I don't have to endure hurt until the pain is numbing.
ACKNOWLEDGE: Feel the throb; see the bruise; expose the wound.

Act as if you have everything under control.
I don't have to disconnect from reality, pretending to be okay.
CONFRONT: Fight the deception, fabrication, and prevarication; leave.

Surrender is weakness. Don't give up what you are doing.
I don't have to faint before giving myself permission to be.
STOP: Be still; be quiet; be meditative.

It is easier to stay with the status quo. It is known and familiar.
I don't have to accept what puts others at ease if I'm ill at ease.
LIVE: Pray for power to perceive, strength to rise, and courage to walk.

REMINDERS

I did not have many plants in my Office, inside my house, or the yards surrounding the house. My mother had many plants inside the house, on the front porch, and in her yards. No doubt she had plants in her workplace. My mother in-law had an incredible "green thumb". Her porches were filled with a variety of green plants – tall, leafy, flowering greenery.

Oh, I did attempt to adorn my space, but the plants did not flourish. Even in my work place, colleagues would rescue that flora that was at the verge of dying. Neglect? Maybe. Bad energy? Probably.

My fortune with plants has improved. Dare I hope that my green plants are flourishing? Each of my plants was a gift, some through inheritance and some as "Get well" wishes. Each plant has a name. Each plant has its place. Plants are my reminders.

I have not kept my plants watered
Enough,
Only when I see the leaves drooping
OR
The leaves turning brown.

I have not visited my plants
Enough,
Only when I feel
Happy
OR
Lost,

And then,
Only if
I remember,
Remember to look.

When I focus, I see the plants.
When I see the plants, I feel the energy.
When I am energized, I recall their names.
When I retain their meanings, I find balance.

Remembering yields illumination.
Remembering becomes something holy.
I named my plants to keep me reminded of life.

Life is in the names:
Nia (Purpose), Kujichagulia (Determination), Umoja (Unity), Harambee (Togetherness), Ujima (Collective Work and Responsibility), Courage (Boldness), M'dear (Mother), Loved (Mother-in-law), and T'vine (Daughter).

As reminders, I will bring three more plants into my home. I am making bequests to me: Spirit (Healing), Shalom (Peacefulness), and Rapture (Joy).

HOLDING ON

Parents died when she was age 8; she held on.
Pregnancy ended with miscarriage when she was 28; she held on.
Husband died when she was age 30; she held on.

Twin daughters she reared alone, many years with temporary jobs, holding on.
Grandchildren, she cherished three, cultivating minds, talents, and brawn; sometimes moving slowly but always holding on.
New Soul Mate renewed joy in her life, but he all too soon expired, despite her grief over lost love again, still she kept holding on.

She was but 40 when cancer attacked her body. But she defied death then.
Fighting all the way, that disease went into remission because she had held on.
Thirteen years later, the "Big C" returned. "Maybe three more years", the doctors said. Despite this grim prognosis, for eleven years, she held on.

The holidays approaching, the news again was bleak, "Two weeks at most," the deadly prognosis came. But it was a joyous Christmas because she kept holding on.

Another year came and went. She was holding on.
Then her grip weakened. "Just make her comfortable. It will be any day now, any day."
She refused to eat.
She declined water.
She rejected medication.

Her gaze was clear but piercing.
Her smile was gentle but fleeting.
Her body was straight but cooling.
No one understood, six days now, how she could still be holding on?

On that sixth day, she uttered but two words, three times she cried out that day.
Lifting from her waist, looking into the distance; speaking loud and clear, she said, "Hold On".

We had talked about the Day of Celebration.
We had penned her wishes for the congregational hymn,
We would sing her song, "Hold to God's Unchanging Hand".

Familiar words of comfort,
"To be absent from the body is to be present with the Lord."
Washed over by sorrow,
The pictures and the memories helped me to hold on.

While death had visited, those left behind must live on.
Sometimes she visited me during waking hours.
She was a persistent spirit seeming to hold on.

It was some years later that she came in a dream to spend some time
with me.
Resting on a low white bed, she was dressed in white.
The dressing gown was of delicate cloth, trimmed in lace, lying in folds.
She was looking loving, looking gentle, looking resolute.

I was standing by her bed; I wore a simple white gown.
We looked upon one another,
Holding back the tears,
I did not know if I could hold on.

I was so unhappy, I told her once again.
I reminded her of my secret shared when we had spoken under an
old oak tree.
She had known already emotions that I had tried to hide.
She had listened and then forcefully told me that I must hold on.

The dream was so real and life-like.
Her eyes looked deep into my own.
Her face conveyed compassion.
Her voice expressed wisdom.

When I woke, I remembered her last words.
The words are ever with me.
She said, "You just hold on".

COMING OVER

Overwhelmed
We fail to focus.
We fail to trust.
We fail to rely on our Life Force.

Overpowered
We are not aware that we are hurting until we notice the self-inflicted injuries.
We are not aware that we are terrorized until we scream, run or pass out.
We are not aware that we are imprisoned until we lose our keys, memory, or mind.

Overcome
We feel breathless.
We feel defeated.
We feel crushed.

Overcoming
We begin.
We begin preparing.
We begin organizing.

Over comer
We anticipate Success.
We recognize Success.
We embrace Success.

Coming Over
We acknowledge that restoration is a progression.
We acknowledge that restoration is a process.
We acknowledge that restoration is a possibility.

Triumph Over
We can claim an alternative mind-set and reject victimization.
We can claim another method and relocate dwelling space.
We can claim a new mission and reclaim Self.

BLESSINGS FROM A SISTER FRIEND

Yesterday, I shared time with a Sister Friend. It was a business appointment, to discuss real estate. The agenda changed. The first order of business was God's.

She entered the living room of my 3-room apartment. The coat rack at the entrance had a serious lean. Let's just admit that it was falling from more than the weight of the coats that hung there. I sat in a wooden, upright, cushioned chair which I had newly acquired next to a dumpster. My Sister Friend plopped down on my old, reupholstered, broken- down couch. She nearly fell as if she could not take another step. On her way to my place, Sister Friend had received bad news: one of her closest friends had died.

Sister Friend sat across from the wall where my family pictures were hanging. Each person peering from within a frame knew my Sister Friend. Did she see them there, looking back at her?

The sun shined through opened blinds, unfiltered by draperies or curtains. Thriving plants could be seen from every part of my living room, plants erected upon marble and ceramic topped stands which my departed mothers once owned. Sister Friend had known them too. Was she aware of the life on view?

In one corner was a "boom box" next to small stacks of tapes and compact discs. Music could be playing with just a touch of a button. The back wall was a reminder of the continuity of life: a mounted collection buttons, organized by each of the 4 members of my family – some historic, some funny, some serious… all memorable.

Contact paper covered the top of an old book case standing below the button collage. Adorning the top shelf was my collection of elephants – all gifts celebrating my sisterhood in Delta Sigma Theta Sorority, Inc. Sister Friend also wore the "Delta" symbol. The shelves below were filled with an assortment of reading materials. There were hardbacks, paperbacks; Christian texts, reference books, variously translated Bibles, and scrapbooks. Did Sister Friend discern that knowledge and wisdom were abounding in this space?

I believed that Sister Friend knew that she was welcome here. If just for a little while, she could just be herself; she could just be. My friend is a fast talker. She was filled up. I listened. I allowed her to pour it all into my cup.

She honored me. Conversing through her pain, she remembered to call me by my "given" name. Each instance that she uttered my nick name, "Max", but then she quickly corrected herself and used my newly declared desired title, "Maxine". I was grateful.

She trusted me. One of the most accomplished, boldly courageous, and well respected women I know, she undressed before me. Exposing her fears, anxieties and hopes, she doubtlessly knew that I would hear, understand, and convey words that would provide covering, consolation and comfort. I was grateful.

S*he awakened me.* The words from her mouth articulated emotions with which I was so familiar, but had dared not speak aloud. Because it was less threatening to my psyche, I try to be dispassionately analytical, even about emotions. Sister Friend said, "I don't know why I always come to you with all of my stuff. You are such a blessing to me."

She comforted me. Expressing her love and admiration for my departed Mama, we both were reminded that some friendships never die. Sister Friend then questioned, lamented, and moaned about the loss of friends, family and self.

I saw in her a reflection of me. The anxieties were so familiar. I, too, have felt the need to be in control of everything, as if that control would guarantee safety and love.
For a moment I was taken back to another place in time: I relived the pain of abandonment, the fear of loneliness, the paralysis from panic, and the anxiety in a life filled with busyness.

I softly said to us, "We are not God. We each are God's Child. We are not alone. We will live." I needed that reminder.

Sister Friend was such a blessing to me.

A HEALING PATH

I kept going down the same path. The path stretched beyond what my eyes could see. I was mesmerized. Occasionally, another road would converge with this path, creating a fork in the road. Sometimes I paused to peer down the adjoining road which, to my eyes, seemed to come to a dead end. Uncomfortable venturing on a road that I had not experienced, I kept traveling the familiar path, even while knowing that there were holes along the way. I figured that if I jumped over or moved carefully along the edges, I would stay on my feet the next time.

However, as I proceeded, the holes became wider, deeper, more numerous and in varied locations along the path. Despite, or was it because of, my familiarity with the path, I would become distracted and fall into a hole. I fell again and again and again. Over time I eventually would climb out. But after a while, I bruised my knees, not to mention my ego; I sprained my ankle, not to mention my self-confidence; I strained my neck, not to mention my outlook; I injured my back, not to mention my mental state; and I broke my leg, not to mention my spirit. It became clear that I needed another way of avoiding the holes. I stood still for a moment.

Evaluating the situation, I decided that I would identify the holes by name: status, denial, shame, pride, hurt and fear. I had pursued status - career, position, income. I had denied that which I valued – faith, family, and friendships. I had concealed what was probably detectable anyway – illness, loneliness, and unhappiness. I had confused pride with arrogance, pretense and vanity. I had developed a high tolerance for abuse – slaps in the face, stabs in the back and kicks in the butt (all figuratively speaking). I had worried, agonized, and fainted rather than confront the truths of human frailty – duplicity, infidelity, and disloyalty.

Desiring to no longer fall into holes, I ventured this time down the other road at the fork. There were no holes on this new path. This road had several hills, but there were no holes. There were divine substitutions: mercy for status, awareness for denial, honor for shame, grace for pride, serenity for hurt, and love for fear.

I stayed on my feet. I had found a healing path.

Walking Differently

You have made known to me the path of life; you will fill me with joy in your presence, with eternal pleasures at your right hand.
Psalm 16:11 (NIV)

And my God will meet all your needs according to his glorious riches in Christ Jesus.
Philippians 4:19 (NIV)

Attempting to manage my recovery from an array of orthopedic ailments and from major depression, I pursued new forms of physical exercises, exercises which were different than the kick boxing, the high impact aerobics, and the cardiovascular and weights machines which I previously enjoyed. I turned to aquatic exercises.

At age 4, my cousin and I almost drowned in my uncle's backyard pool. We might have jumped in, or maybe we fell. I remember the water over my head, under my feet, all around. I was scared. I could not stand up. I could not breathe. The memory is vivid. At age 59, I decided that I would learn to swim. This would be the fifth time I had taken swimming lessons. My instructor was experienced and patient. She told me, "Swimming is about more than swimming." I heard her words, but I did not understand their meaning.

My instructor said to me, "As you practice, you will become comfortable in the water and comfortable with your ability to swim. You will not panic; you will be able to breathe. I thought, "I must be courageous."

My instructor told me, "We will work every part of your body, increase your heart rate, and build up your muscles. I thought. "I must be strong. "

My instructor explained to me, "We will break down the components. You must remember all of the pieces which we will then put together. "I thought, "I must be focused"

During the first lesson, the instructor and I talked about my swimming history and my reason for learning to swim. For three weeks I walked in the pool, my feet touching the floor: I performed a variety of steps, kicks and strides with my feet; I repeated various strokes with my arms; I practiced a new rhythm for breathing while I was gaining control of the water. I had yet to put my face in the water. My fear subsided.

As I walked through the water, my instructions were to hold my head high, look straight ahead, lengthen my body, tighten my abdominal muscles, tuck my hips under, and move my legs from the hips. I supplemented swimming lessons with "Sit and Fit" classes twice a week, training my core muscles. When I lay out in the water, I would maintain the same posture. My muscles became stronger.

49

Between the weekly lessons, I practiced four to five days each week. My instructor said that I had mastered the necessary techniques. With practice, I would be swimming laps non-stop. That would take more time.

In the beginning, my "swims" were quite short, broken up by longer periods of stopping in order to stand back up in the pool and catch my breath. I blew out air, "assumed the correct position" and, "collected" myself. I would swim again and again – six times from end to end. I kept trying. The intervals gradually reduced and I could swim half a lap before I stood. Despite knowing that at no point would the water be over my head when I stood, I could not make it fully across the pool without standing up, just to check. I think that if I relax, while concentrating on the techniques, eventually I will swim a full lap without taking a break. I will believe.

I recognized the similarity of learning to swim and learning to walk. Properly positioned legs, feet and toes kept me up; strong reaching arms propelled me forward; head upon lengthened neck with downward chin drove me forward and gave me direction; steady rhythms of inhaling and exhaling allowed me to breathe. Encouragement from my instructor and the experienced swimmers kept my trying. Both learning to swim and learning to walk engage the body, mind and spirit.

PRAYER JOURNEY

I was
Angry, Outraged, Enraged!
Victimized, Traumatized, Paralyzed.
Yelling, Screaming, Crying
Is anybody listening?

God Grant Me
The SERENITY to accept the things I cannot change:
DEATH
My Daddy, My Mama, My Past

I AM
Survivor, Over Comer, Victor

I was
Scared, Unnerved, Terrified!
I feel so embarrassed, guilty, ashamed, and remorseful.
Hiding, Pretending, Ignoring and Denying
Can somebody make the "elephant" leave the room?

God Grant Me
The COURAGE to Change the things I can
RELATIONSHIPS
With my children, with my spouse, with my Self

I AM
Hopeful, Joyful, Peaceful

I was
Confused, Unfocused, Undisciplined!
Disorganized, Disillusioned, Diseased
Mindless, Clueless, Meaningless
Who will stay with me?

God Grant Me
The WISDOM to know the difference:
SURRENDER
Ask my God; Trust my God; Obey my God

I AM
Stating, Standing, Stepping

My Prayer granted by God
AMEN.

FACING ME

For many years, for decades, decades, I did not, would not look in a mirror. Really, it is quite easy... not to look... I would look at my eyes, my skin, my teeth, my lips, my nose and my chin. But, I would not gaze upon the whole face. I avoided the complete picture. As I progressed through therapy, I began to peer into a mirror – to "sneak a peek".

I was detached. Sometimes I would see my twin gazing at me; other times I would see my mother watching me; at times I would see a face which I imagined as my father's glaring back. Then there were those times that a stranger stared straight at me. After what seemed like a long time, I finally was able to face the mirror and fix my eyes upon the visage that faced me.

For me, looking into a mirror is a very conscious and deliberate act. I avoided mirrors because I wanted to avoid facing me. Perhaps it was a secret I did not want divulged. Perhaps it was a disgrace I did not want unveiled. Perhaps it was a skeleton that I did not want revealed.

I am about to undertake an archeological venture. I wonder what I will discover as I go along on this "dig". I am prepared to meet new parts of me – admission; to acknowledge crude parts of me – acceptance; and to understand puzzling parts of me – confrontation.

It is time for facing me.

WHEN WE LOSE OUR WAY

It was the big joke in my family. I was forever getting lost. Even with a map and written directions, I could not seem to find my way to a given destination, at least not without making at least one wrong turn – either left or right, a back turn or a circular turn. I have lost my car in a parking garage and in the parking lot of a sprawling shopping mall.

Trapped in the back seat of the car on many a lost adventure, when we set off for a new place, my children would ask, "Mama, do you know how to get to where we are going?" I would try to play it off, but every one knows that being lost is no joke. I have encountered others who, too, had become lost - looking for a street, a city... the perfect job, or a better life. Truth be told, there were times that I not only lost my way to a building, but I felt that I lost my way in life.

When we lose our way, do we just keep going?

Do we assume that eventually we will arrive at the place that we want to go? We just don't know when. Sometimes we do not know exactly where. Often we are not certain about the reason for the journey.

Do we suppose that we will recognize the correct street when we see it? We are certain that we will come upon a familiar landmark that will tell us that we have arrived "There". We assert, "We can not define it; we can not describe it; but when we see it we will know."

Do we tell ourselves that "There" is just down the street and around the corner? We've just got to figure out what street, which corner... maybe it's the next one...maybe.

Do we even pause, or do we choose to keep on moving... stepping, running, driving on, full steam ahead, going somewhere... anywhere?

Do we consider that we may have made an error somewhere along the way?

Do we shake off the thought, more than once, that perhaps we are lost? Reaaally lost.

Do we become inattentive or do we ignore the clearly posted signs: CAUTION, WRONG WAY, DEAD END, and STOP. Eventually, we become aware that something is terribly wrong because we now find ourselves on a winding, bumpy, barren, and desolate side road.

Do we become flustered when the journey involves unexpected detours, delays, diversions or distractions?

Journey is defined as travel or passage from one place to another. There are maps, computerized generated directions, and advice from another person who appears to know her way around the neighborhood in which we are lost. A trip may be physical – from home to school, mental – from depression to elation, emotional – from sadness to happiness, or spiritual – from church membership to Christian discipleship. All four facets are part of the journey called life.

When we lose our way, we can ask for directions. Spiritually speaking, we may

Acknowledge that we are lost: acknowledgement is a showing of gratitude.
> **Thank** God for the discernment.

Assume the surrender position: knees bent, body prostrate, head bowed, heart humbled, hands faced up. In total submission -
> **Honor** God for the deliverance.

Sit. Be still. Stay awake and stay alert. Shed: the tears and the fears. See arrival in the mind's eye, safe arrival. Sojourn awhile: pray, meditate, breathe.
> **Trust** God to fulfill the desires of our hearts.

Search: Seek the questions. Recognize the answers when they come – perhaps in a book, perhaps in a song, perhaps in a hug. Have the compassion and the courage to heal the hurts that are among us and the emptiness that is within us.

Allow God to birth through us a new creation.

Know. The directions are within grasp. They lay unwrapped, unopened, unread, hidden in plain view. Let us look in the Book called Bible: study and receive wisdom; research and find guidance; read the stories of Jacob, Joshua, and Joseph; of Claudia, Lydia and Priscilla - reflect and obtain inspiration. Forget not the testimonies, others and our own – hear and heed.

Obey God.

Know. Let there be not a scintilla of doubt. With love, joy, peace, patience, kindness, goodness, faithfulness, gentleness and self-control, know that we will find our way.

Praise God!

A U-TURN

I read the Book of Isaiah
Then walked away from a 29 year government career - **Denial**

I read the Book of Psalms
Then walked away from directorship of an agency - **Pride**

I read the Book Proverbs
Then walked away from my residence of 24 years - **Fear**

I read the Book of Daniel
Then walked away from an illusionary marriage - **Doubt**

So that I could live, I made a U-turn and walked away.

I found that it was not sufficient to simply walk away.
Changing direction ...

I walked to **Acceptance.**

I walked to **Humility.**

I walked to **Love.**

I walked to **Trust.**

REVEALING A DIAMOND

I began therapy to learn how to "fix" my family; yes, I was a true co-dependent. To my surprise, I learned so much more. I uncovered an "elephant" in my family room; I unearthed my buried emotions; I unmasked my persona; I exposed my true self. I tried to run away, more than once. In time, I would crawl back and finally commit to doing the hard work required in therapy. My blessing was in having a Bible-toting therapist whose mission was to be a vessel for God's healing. God ordered my steps to her door. She guided me to a profound, life-saving revelation.

She taught me
      to recognize the signs of dysfunction.
      to do those things which are caring for my self.
      to name that which I fear and to affirm that which I love.

She showed me
      how to look in the mirror.
      how to hug.
      how to surrender.

She encouraged me
      to praise God.
      to accept that which God allows and that which God bestows.
      to acknowledge God's power.

She instructed me
      how to use her seat as a dartboard. I cursed.
      how to use her shoulder as a pillow. I cried.
      how to use her space as a sanctuary. I claimed.

She helped me:
      to accept my own human-ness.
      to embrace my own piece of the Divine.
      to go deep, even if...no, especially, in the dark.

She tutored me
>how to stay on a healing path even when walking in darkness.
>how to cling to life when confronted with death.
>how to love myself when engulfed in fear.

One layer at a time
>methodically, determinedly, purposefully,
>patiently, gently, lovingly,
>gladly, happily, and joyously

Together, we experienced the revealing of a sparkling, radiant diamond, ME!

DREAMS EMPOWERED
An Affirmation

D is for DETERMINATION. I am determined to do that which is pleasing in God's sight. No matter what others may say or do; although it is sometimes very hard, I am going to hold on to my determination to do the right thing.

R is for RESPONSIBILITY. I accept responsibility for my life. I will study God's Word, I will pray, and I will respect my elders so that I can be all that I can be. I am a gift from God . What I become will be my gift to God.

E is for EMPOWERMENT. I am empowered by God. I am a victor, not a victim. I will not give up when I do not get what I want, when I want it, the way that I want it. God is the source of my power. I know that I can do all things through Christ who strengthens me.

A is for ACTION. I am going to act so that the Divine that is within me will show in all that I say and all that I do. I will let the work that I do in Jesus' name speak for me. I will worship the Lord for Who He is and I will continuously praise Him for what He has done, is doing, and will do in my life.

M is for MESSAGE. I will be a messenger for the Lord, a proclaimer of the Word. In my corner of the world, I will share the message of God the Father who can do anything but fail; God the Son who showed me that love conquers all evil; and God the Holy Spirit who gives me hope for today and tomorrow.

S is for STEPS. I know that I am part of God's Plan. He has a purpose for my life. I want my dream to be in step with His Will. So, I will choose to stand on His Word, fully clothed in the armor of God. I pray that the Lord orders my steps each and every day as I prepare for and then walk into my Season.

TRANSFORMATION

From: Job Security
To: Serenity of Job

From: Managing Change
To: Embracing Renewal

From: Facts and Figures called "Knowledge"
To: Peace and Understanding called "Wisdom"

From: Yearly Resolutions
To: Daily Affirmations

From: Skills worked so hard to develop
To: Gifts received just to nurture

From: External Appearance
To: Internal Alignment

From: Abusive Living
To: Abundant Life

From: Doing
To: Being

From: Pressure
To: Precious

From: Darkness in the Closet
To: Light of the Outdoors

From: Lump of Coal
To: Rock of Diamond

A New Self

IT'S MY DESIRE

To be mindful
- Discerning
- Discriminating

To be purposeful
- Focused
- Fervent

To be faithful
- Believing
- Bona fide

To be peaceful
- Sane
- Serene

To be truthful
- Aware
- Authentic

To be loved
- Valued
- Venerated

To be grateful
- Acknowledging
- Appreciating

To be Whole
- Willing
- Walking

INTO MY SPIRIT

Once, people would come into my spirit, unexpectedly, without warning, lacking permission. Sometimes a relative, sometimes a friend. Although I knew the person and shared a history, the reason for this intrusion was an enigma to me. I did not invite them to visit me.

Immediately I would worry. Their presence was unwelcome, disturbing, and bothersome. They had not been invited, what were they doing here? Sometimes I called to "check" on them; sometimes I called another, and asked if she knew "what was up with this"? What did the visit mean? What was I supposed to do? What things was I to give?

I pondered.

Now, people walk into my spirit, always on schedule, no notice needed, prior authorization granted: relative, friend, stranger encountered on the street; with all I have a connection. They know they are welcome. The reason for the visit is an opportunity for me.

I extend my arms in comfort; join hands so we can pray. A pillow comes from the closet, a place setting from the kitchen; and the Bible from a nearby table. Rest, food and hope are offered. This is just a way-station, but during the period of residency, they become a part of me.

When the stay is over, I thank God for the overflow so I could share the gift the Creator gave to me, an unconditional love that's merciful and free. It is an awesome privilege and responsibility to minister to others. My task is to stay focused, balanced, and whole, for I never know when, why, or who next will come walking into my spirit.

I prepare.

SOARING!

First professing
Detecting fears
Discerning denial
Divulging guilt
Disclosing shame

Yet preparing
Accumulating materials
Assembling tools
Accruing knowledge
Arranging plans

Then purging
    Releasing unnecessary emotional baggage
    Tossing worn out, ill-fitting garments
    Heaving piled up papers
    Leaving unhealthy people and places

Next positioning
    Building my muscles for strength
    Strengthening my core for balance
    Lengthening my reach for flexibility
    Increasing my endurance for longevity

Now presenting
    Asserting my voice
    Performing my dance
    Writing my story
    Soaring as my new self!

A NEW HOME

As I contemplated moving to another place, I asked myself:

What will be different about my new home?
I will no longer dwell in a place of P-A-I-N.
   That is not how I spell HOME.
I will no longer dwell in a place of F-E-A-R.
   That is not how I spell HOME.
I will no longer dwell in a place of E-N-V-Y.
   That is not how I spell HOME.

Who will I ask for help in finding a new home?
My twin - she told me how she found her dream home.
My Friends -they told me how they knew of a perfect place
My Confidants - they told me how I could turn any place into a
new home.

How will I make the next address my home?
I will color my home with soft hues that hug.
I will adorn my home with pictures and objects that smile.
I will furnish my home with furniture that sings.

I decided that my new home would be a place where I would have new experiences
New Clarity
New Possibilities
New Restoration

WALKING OUT OF HERE

...I remind you to fan into flame the gift of God, which is in you through the laying on of my hands. For God did not give us the spirit of timidity, but a spirit of power, of love and of self-discipline. (2 Timothy 1:6-7)

Denial is a form of hiding. Sometimes it feels safe. Oft times it feels comfortable. Nearly always it feels familiar. Never does it feel authentic. Denial is a place where I no longer wish to be. I'm walking out of here!

I am walking out of here because I want to...
> LIVE
> Exist, survive, and subsist: to breathe
> Endure, suffer, and undergo: to survive
> Experience, continue, and persist: to last
> Be present, be real, and be here: to be

I am walking out of here because I want my life to be characterized by ...
> FEARLESSNESS
> Fortitude, determination, will, will power, resolve
> Strength, stamina, staying power, resilience, tenacity
> Boldness, bravery, daring, heroism, valor
> Grit, audacity, nerve, purpose, spirit

I am walking out of here because I want to experience joy...
> EVERY DAY
> I am learning more about how to live.
> I am exercising the traits of fearlessness.
> I am remembering the power of choice.
> I am embracing the power of the Divine within.

God's love has brought me to a place of serenity, courage and wisdom. Out of obedience, I share this new understanding.

Epilogue

But now, this is what the LORD says- he who created you, O Jacob, he who formed you, O Israel: "Fear not, for I have redeemed you; I have summoned you by name; you are mine.

When you pass through the waters, I will be with you; and when you pass through the rivers, they will not sweep over you. When you walk through the fire, you will not be burned; the flames will not set you ablaze.

For I am the LORD, your, God, the Holy One of Israel, your Savior; I give Egypt for your ransom, Cush and Seba in your stead.

Since you are precious and honored in my sight, and because I love you, I will give men in exchange for you, and people in exchange for your life.

Do not be afraid for I am with you; I will bring your children from the east and gather you from the west.

I will say to the north, 'Give them up!' and to the south, 'Do not hold them back.' Bring my sons from afar and my daughters from the ends of the earth –everyone who is called by my name, whom I created for my glory, whom I formed and made.

Forget the former things; do not dwell on the past.

See, I am doing a new thing!"

Isaiah 43:1-7, 18 -19(a)

About the Author

After surviving a stroke and experiencing several fainting episodes, *Maxine Bigby Cunningham* embraced a holistic approach to getting back on her feet and learning to walk again. She gave nearly 30 years of service with the US Department of Housing and Urban Development before beginning a second career with grassroots nonprofit organizations. She earned degrees from Goucher College and the Maxwell School of Citizenship and Public Affairs at Syracuse University. Her writings have appeared in publications of NAMI Metropolitan Baltimore, Inc. and the Maryland State Poetry and Literary Society.

Made in the USA
Middletown, DE
03 February 2015